JOYFUL STREETS

Ten Years of Handmade Parade

Linda Green and Andrew Kim

Written by Linda Green and Andrew Kim

Foreword by John Fox

Sub editor and designer: Mike Barrett, frogsdesign

Photo selection: Andrew Kim, Mike Barrett and Ian Hodgson

Editing and proofing: Rebecca Dearden

Front cover
Squid by Kerith Ogden with Blowjangles (band); photo by Chris Ratcliffe

Back cover
Musk Ox by Andrew Kim; photo by Darren Fleming

Inside cover
Stilt-walking class by Spyros Andreopoulos and Maisha Kungu;
photo by Andrew Kim

ISBN: 978-1-9998783-0-6

Contents

Why do we parade?

foreword by John Fox

PARADES come in all shapes and sizes, in sequins and blisters. In March 1849, hundreds of starving people walked from Louisburgh in County Mayo, Ireland, to a mansion where dinner was served to their 'Board of Guardians'. Denied food and certificates of destitution, about 100 participants died on the return. Every year since 1988 this famine march has been symbolically re-enacted.

In 1971 in New York, the Bread and Puppet theatre company paraded with remarkable giant puppets to protest the Vietnam war. They also celebrated Halloween and Independence Day.

At Easter, throughout Hispanic culture, thousands of pilgrims, local people and tourists have for centuries followed processions to celebrate the Passion of Christ. In Malaga, one swayed, like a purposeful whale, through a massive crowd, as a hundred men perspiring in tight black suits and ties carried a huge glassed shrine of a beautifully carved replica of the Virgin Mary.

Contemporary lantern parades originated in Ulverston, Cumbria in 1983 through a prototype of Welfare State International (WSI). The parade is now an annual town event. One September evening, before autumn darkens, hundreds take to the streets with their sculptural candlelit lanterns made at home from willow and tissue paper. In an entirely non-commercial celebration of place, family and community, the event has become for some a special secular rite of passage.

Now extensively copied world-wide, it was inspired by a Buddhist/Shinto procession experienced by WSI in Japan in 1982. Big drums beat from a high mountain temple.

Phalanxes of muscular, loin-clothed men merged down a forest road carrying huge carved lanterns with colourful illuminated paintings of demonic gods. High on each frame, a small boy was strapped in as if in the crow's nest of a sailing ship. When the lanterns were launched into the harbour, the village fishing fleet was blessed.

Parades come little and big. The traditional rush-bearing church processions in the Lake District, England, are tiny. Thirty or so costumed children, their mothers, a priest and a silver band parade through the parish with banners, reeds and decorated baskets. They contrast with Macey's commercial Thanksgiving Day Parade in New York when giant copycat inflatables and paraders draw thousands to watch and consume possibly the world's largest parade. 2017 was its 90th year.

Clearly, we must parade. From funerals to carnivals and gatherings in between, from Gay Pride to St Patrick's Day, we mark solidarity. We commemorate, show off, protest and reinforce occasions with friends, fans, religionaires, bands, soldiers, politicos and family.

My favourite parades celebrate joy with excess. Here, Handmade Parade excels. Inside their creative cauldron in Hebden Bridge in Yorkshire, you become a child again. In a laughing frenzy of cardboard and paint, glue and ideas, staple guns, scissors and gaffer tape, a carnival cornucopia materialises. A randy dragon, a bog-eyed camel, a bored tortoise and a tranquil stork play with a paper politician and a weary sludge gulper. Rendering chaos, giant dentures bite the bum of recalcitrant hedgehog until an elderly hippo and a wise green man take control, play resonant horns and lead everyone to sunshine outside.

So, the parade starts, the cycle perpetuates and the sun returns.

That's why we parade.

John Fox MBE is an artist, poet and cultural provocateur. His company Welfare State International (1968-2006) re-invented influential prototypes of fire shows, site specific theatre, lantern parades and street music. His current company, Dead Good Guides with Sue Gill, trains celebrants in secular rites of passage and seeks a role for art that weaves it more fully into our lives.

Introduction by founder and artistic director Andrew Kim

HEBDEN BRIDGE is a jewel of a town set in the narrow green valleys of the South Pennines in West Yorkshire, England. Although the population is just 5000, Hebden Bridge has become known for its independent shops, alternative culture and as the home of many creative businesses and professionals.

In 2006, Kathy and I had just married and decided to base our new lives and our new puppet company, Thingumajig Theatre, in Hebden Bridge. Kathy is Yorkshire born and bred, and I had moved here from the USA where I'd spent several years making puppets, plays and parades. As our company's work developed from its Hebden Bridge base, we were finding work far afield but we couldn't find any opportunities to share our work locally. At the same time, we got to know several artists in the area who were also experiencing the same problem. As someone new to the Calder Valley and to the country, I thought a parade could be just what we all needed. What better way to meet your neighbours than to make some art, put on some stilts and dance down the streets?

Teaming up with kindred spirits Jude Wadley and Mel Rix of HEADS (a participatory arts organisation based in Hebden Bridge) who came on board to manage the fundraising and production elements of the parade, we started speaking to local artists, musicians and event organisers. We found a temporary home, thanks to the generous loan of an unused industrial space by a local commercial landlord, and we were off and away.

I wanted to introduce a slightly different way of making a parade and so borrowed some organising tools from some of the events I'd worked on in the States. From the very first parade in Hebden Bridge, we have held to two rules: no written words or logos and no motorised vehicles (except mobility scooters). These are principles borrowed from the Fremont Summer Solstice Parade in Seattle.

The first rule assures that ours is never a commercial parade. There can be no advertising—it's about the art and the people who make it, not about a product or a service or a company. It also marks a difference from other carnival parades where participants often represent groups identified by written signs. I wanted to have a parade where people's creativity was the central focus. In our parade, participants don't represent their school or church or sports team or political cause or place of employment; they are there to show and perform the costume they've made themselves. They are identified artistically by the parade section they've chosen to be in. So, they may be with the dung beetle section or the flying pig section, making their costumes next to friends, neighbours, strangers of all ages who have also chosen to be a dung beetle/flying pig. Because— here's the secret: the parade is not about the parade. It's about creating the space where people have the opportunity and the occasion to make something together that's big and colourful (and sometimes messy)

and always better because we're working together. We are making space for our creativity and building community as a matter of course.

The second rule assures that it is a people-sized parade moving at the pace of the youngest walking participant. We want to make a space where children's art is as celebrated as the giant puppets.

Each year, we start the process with a Spark Day, an open meeting where we invite anyone in our community to say what they would like to see in this year's parade. The conversation swings from topical local issues to whimsical costume or performance ideas. We push and pull these ideas into a few favourite themes then turn this over to the parade staff. The lead artists and the artistic director then have a series of design meetings to shape the most dynamic parade we can from these favourite ideas. Once we choose the theme, we break up into parade sections, which are like the chapters of a book. Each lead artist takes a section and designs it with the feedback of the team. Each section will have some central giant puppets and/or floats, alongside several ensembles supporting the theme and at least one costumed music band. These ideas are drawn onto a storyboard. I borrowed this system of generating and designing themes from the MayDay Parade by In the Heart of the Beast Puppet and Mask Theatre in Minneapolis.

When the parade participants come to the workshop for the first time, they are introduced to this storyboard. They then choose which ensemble they would like to be in. They go to the section table where the lead artist, with the help of interns and volunteers, shows them some prepared example costumes and gives them all the materials, tools and instruction they need to make their own costume. Some people only come for one two-hour session, most come for between three and five sessions. Some come even more. Often parents come back on their own after their children's costumes are done so they don't look out of place in their street clothes. Everyone is in costume in our parade; it's certainly not just for kids!

We hold three weeks of open workshops every Saturday and Sunday and Tuesday and Thursday afternoon. The workshops are free, but we encourage donations.

We also hold parade classes in stilt-walking, samba drumming, dance and street theatre. We find this is a good way to attract a wider pool of participants and infuse more performance into the parade. The Handmade Samba Band, our in-house community drumming group started by Mitch Oldham for our second parade is much in demand throughout the year playing at parades and events across the north of England. More recently, our stilt walkers are helping to support more and more of our other events.

Our parade is the creation of our town. It is also a crucible for all the experience and influences of the artists who have helped shape it. In addition to the two events in the States I mentioned, my work with Bread and Puppet has inspired the use of giant puppets, cardboard and pageantry. Welfare State International has been a huge influence for many of our team, especially in their work with making big, accessible spectacle with bamboo and willow withies. We also owe a great deal to the dazzle, dance and drumming we've learned from West Indies inspired carnivals.

And we owe a great debt of gratitude to the visiting guest artists who have come to help us with our parades from across the UK, Ireland, USA, Denmark, Sweden, Spain, Italy, Bulgaria, the Czech Republic and Korea and companies Cardboardia (Russia) and Motus Terrae (Greece). Each brought new variations of creating art and performance with participants and hopefully took a little bit of Handmade Parade magic to sprinkle into their community.

We make this book to mark 10 years of our parade. For those of you who have made a mask, cleaned a paint brush, banged a drum and danced down the street with us, thank you so much for sharing your very best with us. Haven't we done well? Shall we do it again?

For those of you who are further away, discovering us from these photos and these stories, welcome! Trust that when you create space and invite your community in, when you listen to and support each other as artists, when you are open to and grateful for receiving help, there's the possibility for great joy and beauty.

Our Vision

HANDMADE PARADE is a collection of artists and event makers who create stunning community-generated celebrations. With a spirit of openness, using accessible techniques and affordable materials, we create spaces and opportunities to encourage as many people as possible to make the best art possible.

We believe that the journey is as critical as the destination. The act of gathering people to prepare for an event provides the occasion for a community to come together in its most creative and generous self.

Inspired by traditions of carnival, circus and puppetry, we believe that masquerade is a vital vehicle for us to recognise the awe, beauty and joy in the world around and in each other. It's necessary to occasionally grab ones family, friends and familiars and claim the right to dance down the centre of your own street and be applauded for doing so. We're here to say, go on, we'll set it up for you. Wouldn't it be better with a little more sparkle and a samba band?

We aim for excellence. We are not about numbers but richness of experience. Whether in our signature giant puppets or in the details of a participant's costume, we set ourselves high standards and make space for the artist inside everyone.

Beauty for us is not only in the level of finish but in the energy of intent and freedom of expression.

We believe a community celebration can only be successful with a spirit of giving. We recognise that people want to help; people want to be a part of something bigger than themselves. When we welcome everyone with whatever they can give, we find they often have more to offer than they realise and this is exactly the point.

Andrew Kim

Hebden Bridge
Handmade Parade

2008

Deluge of Delights

Produced by HEADS and Thingumajig Theatre

Director: Andrew Kim

Lead Artists: Kerith Ogden, Alison Duddle, Jonny Quick

Organisers: Mel Rix, Jude Wadley

I
N OUR VERY FIRST Hebden Bridge Handmade Parade, water was our theme. We live in a valley carved by rivers. Rivers powered industry and the canal connected us to the world and it's our 500-year-old bridge across the river that gave us our name.

The parade started with a pair of clowning geese pace-setters (Kathy Kim and Michelle Silcox) who warmed up the audience for the parade to follow. These geese were inspired by the bossy geese who live in our canal marina and often claim the roads around it. We had no idea that this would be the start of a tradition: every Hebden Bridge Handmade Parade has been led by Kathy and Michelle in characters to fit the theme.

The first section featured Alison Duddle's mysterious Water Bearers followed by fish kites, frogs and midges. Kerith Ogden's second section featured water birds: ducks, geese and a massive section of kingfishers. She made a giant heron puppet – the only giant puppet we still have and use 10 years later.

The third section, led by Jonny Quick, started with narrow boats. Concerned that there wouldn't be a big take-up with this costume, he introduced pirates on narrow boats. But, as pirates do, they soon took over the section.

The final section, designed by Andrew Kim, was about the rain that brings growth. This featured a Rain Queen and painted umbrellas inspired by New Orleans second line parades and ended with rainbow flags.

Parade music was provided by Peace Artistes, Beatlife and Mbackeh Darboe with a song written by Kathy Kim led by Calder Valley Voices.

Just what Hebden Bridge needed

Jude Wadley

JUDE WAS THERE at the beginning of the first Handmade Parade and has been involved most years since. She was working at local arts organisation HEADS when the idea of the parade was first mooted. She said: "I'd always wanted to do a parade in Hebden, so when I heard that Andrew Kim was looking for people to partner with, I was like, yes, let's do it.

"When we were in that first workshop space and it was really busy and the space was filling up with colourful costumes, it was starting to feel special. People were looking at the forecast and saying it was going to rain but it didn't. It has never rained on our parade. We've had a bit of drizzle in the line-up and downpours in the park, but never on the parade.

"That first parade was just phenomenal and you could tell as you went down the street that people were loving it and as soon as we'd done it we said, let's do it again."

One of Jude's roles over subsequent years was as an outreach co-ordinator. She explained: "It's about giving people that opportunity to get involved, people who might not come to a public workshop for all sorts of reasons. To be able to go to them and give them something that's appropriate in a place that they're comfortable with, that's the beauty of outreach, because not everyone can cope with that frenetic, noisy workshop environment. It's about doing something that's tailor-made for the group we're working with and their abilities and needs.

"Sometimes, it's too much for people who are feeling vulnerable and they just make something and come and watch the parade, because being in it wouldn't suit them. Their artwork might be site decoration or someone else will carry it for them, but they can still be part of it.

"My highlight was when we did outreach work at Hebden Vale, with a lady in her nineties who made an umbrella. On parade day she was there with her daughter, granddaughter and great-grandson. She was in her wheelchair and her great-grandson was in his buggy and there were the four generations of one family who wouldn't have come to the parade if great-grandma hadn't been involved, and to me, there's nothing that's topped that."

Jude has also worked as producer of the parade. She said: "Being a producer has huge responsibilities but there's also huge satisfaction in knowing that all your hard work has paid off. Everything you've been working on for months may only last a few hours on the day but the memories stay in people's minds for much longer. Those memories live on."

But it's been taking part in the dance ensemble in the parade, that has been the most fun. "I'm much happier dancing down the street than running about being responsible. The dance rehearsals are huge fun and there's so much silliness in preparing for the parade that, by the time parade day comes around, you've kind of filled up with all the joy of making it and you take that with you onto the streets. You take the lid off the fun and just let it out and share it with the crowds."

2009

Glorious Garden Party

Produced by HEADS and Thingumajig Theatre

Director: Andrew Kim

Lead Artists: Kerith Ogden, Dave Young,
Alison Duddle

Organisers: Mel Rix, Jude Wadley

FOR THE SECOND Hebden Bridge Handmade Parade, we took the theme of gardens. The parade's pace-setters were singing garden gnomes. The first section, led by Kerith Odgen, featured a rotating sun followed by plant pots, gardeners and a big section of slugs around a giant snail. This was followed by Dave Young's section of ants, ladybirds and a giant walking, smoke-shooting spider. Alison Duddle's section included bees, a Queen Bee, flowers and butterflies and the parade ended with Andrew Kim's section of the bounty of the garden: fruits, vegetables, flowers and a giant, ancient tree puppet.

This year, we taught parade classes as well as the open costume workshops. Mitch Oldham started our in-house band, Handmade Samba Band, Andrew taught stilt-walking, Alison taught giant puppet-making.

Fran Sierevogel, Sue Walpole and Catherine Sweeney taught workshops at local schools and community centres.

Calder High students created a dance finale to welcome the sun and street bands included:

Handmade Samba, Peace Artistes, Beatlife, Slick Stick Sambastics, and Carnival Crew Tees Valley who provided drums and dancers.

And the beat goes on

Mitch Oldham

ASK PEOPLE about the Handmade Parade and one of the first things they'll mention is the music. Whether it's the power of Drum Machine, the fun of Skiband or the revamped 90's tunes of Mr Wilson's Second Liners, the different styles of music blend perfectly in the parade. And at the heart of that is the Handmade Samba Band, the house band for the Handmade Parade, which has been part of it all from 2009.

Its leader, Mitch Oldham, explains: "The style of music is Brazilian street carnival music. It's intended to make people dance. It's very uplifting music. Within a parade, this is the ideal sort of music because it's exciting and it really animates everything that's happening around. It's very joyous.

"The beauty of samba is there's something really simple rhythmically that people can play, all the way up to something complicated, and it all fits together. Things can be simplified or can be made more challenging, so

anyone can join, anyone can feel they are immediately part of the parade band.

"So, from my point of view, the idea is that I can help people develop their confidence. If they've been involved in this sort of thing before I can help them develop their skills to a higher level and that's my main aim really, to bring this community band together. It's made up of people who are not professional players but are trying to aspire to be the best they can. My job is to try to make sure they are playing at the best of their ability."

And a particularly important aspect for Mitch is bringing on complete novices and boosting their confidence. "We run all year as a band but for the Handmade Parade we have people come who only want to play in the parade once a year or who have never played before and they'll come to me and say "I'm nervous, I've tried instruments before and I've not been able to read the music. I don't know what I'm doing."

"But the great thing is people can

come without an instrument, without any specialist knowledge and just join in. It's up to me to boost their confidence by getting them to play something simple first of all and if that's where they want to stay, that's fine, or they might want to be more challenged. That's the point of a community band, we allow everyone to play.

"And on parade day, when we have our costumes on, all in the style of our parade section, I get this wonderful thing of being able to stand at the front and conduct it but then look back towards the whole band and see everybody. There are thousands of people on the streets and there are certain places in Hebden when we come around a corner and you know that it's going to be really special. People are cheering us, they are always incredibly responsive. It's amazing. And to be able to stand back and watch that happening, is wonderful."

Mitch plays at different events across the country but he feels the Handmade Parade is very special.

"One thing that constantly surprises me every single year is the level of excellence and the high standard of everything involved, from the tiniest little puppets, all the way to the biggest animations and the music that's involved. This is the thing that's incredible, Hebden Bridge is only a small town, five or six thousand people. To have something of such high quality here is really special."

2010

Hop, Skip and a Jump

Produced by Handmade Parade CIC

Director: Andrew Kim

Lead Artists: Kerith Ogden, Theo Wickenden, Alison Duddle

Organiser: Rebecca Dearden

THE 2010 PARADE theme was Hop, Skip and a Jump – a celebration of journeys real and imaginary. Intrepid scouts led the parade, followed by stilt-walking Canada geese, designed by Alison Duddle. This first section included migrating animals such as penguins, butterflies, whales, Arctic terns. There was also a pedal-powered hippo by Thingumajig Theatre.

The second section, designed by Theo Wickenden, featured all the ways humans move: cars, planes, horses, boats and a giant pair of feet! The final section, by Kerith Ogden, showed fantastical journeys to outer space (planets, aliens, UFOs) and to the bottom of the sea (deep sea creatures and a giant squid).

Andrew Kim directed a finale pageant with parade participants. Using some of the parade ensembles, masks, cardboard props, giant puppets and a good bit of dancing, we told a simple story of people who, in their rush to get somewhere, have forgotten where they are. Thanks to the help of some cheeky animals and a generous sun ensemble, we are connected back to the beauty of our natural world.

Soozin Hirschumgl from the USA was our guest artist and worked with our stilt-walkers and created a giant stilt-walking puppet.

Parade bands included: Beatlife, Blowjangles, Peace Artistes, Handmade Samba and an ensemble of local musicians who played for the finale pageant.

Growing up with the Handmade Parade The Children

THERE'S A GENERATION of children who have grown-up with the Handmade Parade. Rohan Green was three when he was in the first parade and he has taken part in every one since. Now 13, he considers himself a parade veteran. He said: "over the years, I've been crazy things such as a courgette, a flying machine, a deep-sea diver – walking the entire parade in a wetsuit and flippers – and a tree with a crow's nest.

"My favourite costume was probably the centaur I made for the Myths, Mysteries and Mayhem parade because me and my mum were both in these costumes and we had the horse's legs sticking out behind us and it was really fun to do the parade like that.

"It's such a great opportunity to perform and it's such fun, you have an absolute whale of a time doing it. It's great when you're lining up for the parade because you finally get to see everyone in their costumes and it really feels like, this is it, this is what the Hebden Bridge Handmade Parade is all about. Without the parade, I would never have dressed up as a courgette!"

Other children have developed entirely new skills from being in the parade. Isaac Hughes Dennis, aged 14, loves being on stilts every year.

"There are so many good memories. I think the big one for me would be three years ago when I led the parade as a giant three-foot stilt-walking toucan and I had giant wings that extended about a foot off my arms. It was a fairly windy day, which usually on stilts is absolute hell, but when the wind caught my wings they would swoop and slide and, seeing the looks on people's faces, I think that was the best memory for me.

"The first time I stilted, I was extremely nervous. I remember taking little baby penguin steps and I was thinking I was going to fall, but I didn't. My confidence has grown a lot since then. I think the stilt-walking workshops, and the workshops in general at the Handmade Parade, are a big boost for self-confidence.

"The parade means absolutely everything to me, it's the only place that you can go and get to be creative and be yourself. It's the only place where you can make giant wings or stretch around in PVC trousers on four-foot poles. It's completely brilliant."

Gala Baldacci is another teenager who is grateful for the opportunities the parade has given her. And she remembers clearly her first experience of stilting.

"I thought I would fall over again and again until I got it right but that's not how it works. Everyone's so helpful, I found it a bit difficult at first, I held on to my dad and Travis, one of the instructors, for a good 20 minutes before I let go.

But after a while, it just becomes an extension of your legs and it's so easy that you forget you're on stilts. It's great, I'm definitely a lot more confident now than when I started. I'm still a little bit nervous but I think that's what makes it so much fun. I feel super comfortable doing it now and like a piece of the furniture in the parade. I would never have learnt to stilt without the parade, never in a million years, and that's what's so brilliant. Half the kids in Hebden can stilt now and I think that's a wonderful thing."

2011

Yum! The Fabulous Feast

Produced by Handmade Parade CIC

Director: Andrew Kim

Lead Artists: Dave Young, Alison Duddle, Jonny Quick

Organiser: Rebecca Dearden

THE THEME of this year's parade was Yum! The Fabulous Feast, with an array of mouth-watering art and costumes. The parade was headed by singing dinner ladies who were followed by a section of sweets, doughnuts and junk food and a massive hungry mouth designed by Jonny Quick. This was followed by Alison Duddle's section of seedlings, sunshine and garden delights led by a green earth goddess giant puppet.

Andrew Kim designed the next section about markets which featured fish and a giant fishmonger, market traders, cheese, chicken and eggs and a giant hen by Thingumajig Theatre. The final section, by Dave Young, was the feast: chefs and stilt-walking waiters served up pies and cakes. Dave also made a king-sized lobster and pie complete with mechanical blackbirds.

The parade culminated in a finale performance in Calder Holmes Park, directed by Andrew Kim, in which the hungry mouths were wooed by the allure of sweets and junk food but all was made well again by some friendly animals, the earth goddess, rays of sunshine and a giant chicken.

Music was provided by Beatlife, Blowjangles, Handmade Samba, Skiband, Calder Valley Voices, Rhythmbridge and an in-house brass band led by Peadar Long.

A volunteer for life

Louise Heppleston

JUNE, for me, has become a month whose soundtrack is rain and when sun does not feature. Why? Because you'll find me inside the Handmade Parade workshop, cleaning paint pots, cutting out quite tricky cardboard shapes and making sure the pre-recycled gets re-recycled. This is the lot of the Handmade Parade volunteer.

I don't have the artistic skills of the artists and can only watch, awestruck, as Andrew's organisational skills ensure it runs to clockwork year after year. But as a volunteer, I can play my part in keeping this show on the road and, every year, I return to touch base with the incredible community in which I live. I work in Lancashire (someone has to) and can feel disconnected from my town. The Handmade Parade, especially the workshops, gives me the time and place to talk to and engage with people from all over the valley. I've chatted with the recently bereaved, for whom the parade workshops have been balm to the soul. I've kept children engaged and on task while

their parents work on their own costumes. I've seen those children grow up, returning year after year and becoming more skilled, confident and independent.

Some years I've done my Rapunzel act, sitting up in the roof space sewing multi coloured reams of incredibly slippery fabric into whatever is required by our lead artists. Another trick, which I learned early on gets you double Brownie points as a volunteer, is to make... well, brownies, or any other form of cake, for your fellow volunteers, interns and parade artists. Although trying to make one that is vegan, gluten free AND uses only locally sourced ingredients can stretch one's ingenuity.

It's worth it. The other volunteers are pretty amazing too. I've re-connected with some of the women I did A level art with back in 1987...so good to share memories.

I've also shared my house with an artist from Bulgaria – Plamen you were just great, and thank heavens for Google Translate so I can read your Facebook posts to

stay in touch. Because that's what volunteering is about. Making new connections, rediscovering old ones and strengthening current ones. You may think that cutting out endless wings for Arctic terns or breast plates for scarab beetles is a strange way to spend your summer weekends, but it allows me to chat and be available to so many fascinating and gifted people. Handmade Parade is really good at enabling folk to realise that they possess talents they never knew they had – that moment of realisation, part-way through a costume make, when someone says: 'Oh my, did I really just make that?' is priceless. And no less so because it happens every week, at every workshop.

Those workshops also give me a quiet space to think and contemplate, a couple of hours outside my everyday life and work where, in the safety of the parade workshop, my mind can be calm and I can engage in the moment.

Back in 2012, when I heard my daughter was pregnant, my first thought was, when can my

grandchild reasonably take part in her first Handmade Parade? The answer to that was 2017, when my slightly diffident and none-too-certain four-year-old granddaughter Hollie had the best time ever in the workshops and in her first parade. We like to get the next generation of volunteers in training early.

2012

The Enchanted Wood

Produced by Handmade Parade CIC

Director: Andrew Kim

Lead Artists: Lisa Gort, Kerith Ogden,
Fran Sierevogel

Organisers: Rebecca Dearden and Hannah Merriman

THE DAY BEFORE the scheduled 2012 parade, the train came and wouldn't stop. Hebden Bridge and neighbouring towns in the Upper Calder Valley, suffered severe flooding. We decided to postpone the parade until the following weekend. Following a massive community mopping-up effort, we were ready to go.

The theme was The Enchanted Wood and the parade was split into four sections following the woods through the four seasons. Two new lead artists joined the team: Lisa Gort and Fran Sierevogel. Lisa designed spring with birds, sprouting plants, flowers and a giant hedgehog. Fran's summer section featured a giant green man with trees in formal wear, woodland warriors and shield bugs.

Andrew Kim's autumn session included an autumn leaf dragon, squirrels chasing acorns, tree stilt-walkers chased by lumberjacks and a monster digger. Winter, designed by Kerith Ogden, featured a white stag, a giant boar, howling wolves, owls and skeletons holding skeleton trees.

The parade culminated in a finale performance in which a Trojan hedgehog full of lots of little hedgehogs helped the lumberjacks see the forest through the trees.

Coming just one week on from the floods, our town was awash with colour and music. The parade provided a much-needed boost to community spirit and let the world know we were back and very much open for business.

What a difference ten years makes
Linda Green

I HAD NO IDEA when I strolled into a workshop for the first Handmade Parade in 2008 that I was entering into a lifelong relationship, one which would involve me being chair of Handmade Parade CIC for five years and parading through Hebden Bridge as a crow wearing yellow washing up gloves on my feet!

Relationships like that don't come along very often and I was understandably a little apprehensive at first. My three-year-old son was keen to create a splendid pirate ship and I was somewhat challenged in the making-things-with-my-own-hands department.

I needn't have worried, though. From the moment I walked into the massive warehouse, the three-year-old tugging at my hand, we were made to feel incredibly welcome by the parade artists and, most importantly, made to feel that we were capable of creating something special.

Along the way, I managed to conquer my complete inability to use an industrial-sized stapler and reached the stage where I was actually able to show someone else how to reload one and pass on the golden rule of workshops; never let a working stapler out of your sight.

Small successes maybe, but the sense of belonging, of coming together with the community and being part of something truly magical, is something far bigger than that.

My son has grown-up with the parade, going from toddler to teenager, each year marked with a different costume and creation. I have watched other people's children grow up over the years too, developing new skills, be it stilting, playing in the samba band or devising ever crazier costumes. What they all share is a growing level of confidence in their own abilities and the knowledge that communities have the power to achieve incredible things.

That sense of community was never more evident than after the flood of 22 June 2012. We were just leaving the workshops, the night before the parade, when the flood warning sounded. Nothing could have prepared people for the deluge that was about to hit the town, leaving the streets we were due to parade through the next day under many inches of water.

The decision was taken overnight to postpone the parade and concentrate instead on helping people with the mopping up operation. Fortunately, the costumes and giant makes escaped unscathed but many of the people due to be parading in them and carrying them, were not so lucky.

The town was reeling but the way people pulled together was incredible. That sense of community which had been so evident at the parade workshops was now put to good use helping to get the town back on its feet after the devastation. And rescheduling the parade for the following Saturday was a hugely important part of that. The community needed to show what it was made of and to show off its amazing costumes and creations.

As I strutted along the route in the aforementioned crow costume complete with yellow washing up gloves for feet, the sense of pride I felt in this community had never been stronger.

As I look back at ten years of the parade, there is so much to love about the way the event has embedded itself in the Hebden Bridge calendar. But one of the things I love the most is the fact that you can smile at someone you pass in the street without necessarily knowing their name but knowing that they once rocked a dung-beetle costume alongside you in the parade.

Linda was Chair of Handmade Parade CIC 2010-2015

2013
Myths, Mysteries and Mayhem

Produced by Handmade Parade CIC

Director: Andrew Kim

Lead Artists: Kerith Ogden, Lisa Gort, Fran Sierevogel, Jonny Quick

Organiser: Hannah Merriman

THE 2013 PARADE explored myths connected to the elements of earth, water, fire and air. Jonny Quick led the earth section with trolls, horned beasts, groovy goblins, giant Easter Island heads and a Minotaur. Lisa Gort's water section included mermaids, deep sea creatures, explorers and a giant whale.

Kerith Ogden's fire section was led by a Brigid giant puppet followed by dragon on bikes, fire birds, fire-fighting salamanders and tricksters. Fran Sierevogel's air section featured flying pigs, winged horses and cherubs around a giant heart.

The finale pageant told the story of a clan of trolls and their many failed attempts to stand stones. They were aided by the horned stilt-walking beasts who called forth the four elements. The stones stood and one magically opened and a giant disco ball emerged. The show ended with a community disco.

Outreach artists Thea Soltau, Sarah Terry, Sue Walpole and Jude Wadley created parade art off-site with a dozen school and community groups.

This year's success was in a large part due to the help of four assistant artists – Gil Burns, Bella Lyster, Douglas Thompson and Joanna McGlynn from Galway. American guest artist Duane Tougas created a remarkable set of cardboard-sculpted oversized troll masks.

It's about the ability, not the disability Ruth Richardson

RUTH RICHARDSON is a familiar figure in the Handmade Parade with her wheelchair used as a base for increasingly ambitious creations. But while she may strike those watching as being confident in her wheels, Ruth explained that it was not always the case.

"The first parade I did was Hop, Skip and a Jump, and we were with the migrating whales and penguins. My abiding memory is that I was quite self-conscious about using a wheelchair and, when we rounded the corner by the town hall, there were thousands of people looking at me and I thought, oh my goodness, here I am – and that really helped me with my attitude about using the wheelchair.

"I think the other thing I realised is that it's about the costume and the ability, not about the disability. When children look at what I'm producing, they say, 'Oh, your costume's on wheels', which is brilliant. They all want wheels like me.

"It's made me feel different about using the wheelchair outside the parade because it's about the person and not the disability. That's a big thing to get over, but I think I've cracked it."

Ruth's skills as a maker have also improved significantly over the years and she insists that's down to the talented team of parade artists.

"The section leaders and assistants are tremendous and give me such support because, physically, I can't always realise the stuff that I've got in my head.

"This year I was asked, 'Would you like to be the fisher queen?' And I thought, oh yes, I can wave from the elbow. They gave me the ideas and I ran with it – or wheeled with it, in my case!"

The parade is very much a family affair and many of the special memories for Ruth involve enjoying the event with her grandchildren, who she's watched grow with the parade.

She said: "The parade is very special because we do it as a family group and that's very important that we're all in the same section and we're all involved together. It's not all about the day, it's about the doing it and making it and the laughs that we have along the way.

"It's one of the most important things on the calendar for our family. We can go nowhere in June when the workshops are on."

Like many participants, Ruth has made new friends through the parade workshops and has particularly enjoyed meeting the international visitors. "Just eavesdropping on a Greek and a Russian conversing in fluent English is a good experience!"

And rubbing shoulders with artists and performers has certainly had a positive effect about how she sees her role in the parade. "I think we've all learned that you interact with the spectators and get them involved in what you're doing. Last year, the Christmas tree creation sank on to my shoulders before we got to the end of the road so I was actually holding it up and shouting to the crowd, "we have a design fault", that's the sort of exchange that's all part of the fun. It's not like them and us. It's everybody joining in together and the atmosphere is always tremendous."

2014

Endangerous Expedition

Produced by Handmade Parade CIC

Director: Andrew Kim

Lead Artists: Lisa Gort, Kerith Ogden,
Fran Sierevogel

Event Producer: Hannah Merriman

In our seventh Hebden Bridge Handmade Parade, we wanted to remember and honour endangered and extinct animals. The parade started with a pair of dodo birds made by Thingumajig Theatre. The first section, set in the jungle and designed by Fran Sierevogel, featured tigers, monkeys, toucans and elephants. Andrew Kim's section travelled to the Arctic to find families of polar bears on the move with cases, Arctic foxes, spirit poles and a giant musk ox.

The third section, designed by Lisa Gort, included scorpion warriors, pangolins and camels. The final section, led by Kerith Ogden, featured coral reef dancers, manta rays, sharks and sea turtles, including a giant turtle with a revolving earth on its back.

Handmade Samba Band, Skiband, Northern Lights Street Orchestra, Drum Machine, Dhamak and Beatlife, provided the music along the route to Calder Holmes Park, where they entertained the crowds at the parade finale, along with belly-dancing troupe Kuz-e-kuzza from Halifax and Todmorden Belly Dance.

Mask-maker Susan Albertsen and Helge Jorgensen from Denmark and Alice Barte from Sweden joined our team. Student placements Jessica Imrie and Maeve Black from Liverpool Institute for Performing Arts provided essential help to the team.

The popular CBBC television show Blue Peter paid us a visit and featured us in one of their episodes, Presenter Barney Harwood joined lead artist Fran for a special making session and Fran earned her Blue Peter badge!

Helping makers to shape the Parade
Kerith Ogden

IF YOU ASK PEOPLE to name their favourite Handmade Parade big makes, the chances are they will mention something made by Kerith Ogden.

Kerith has been a lead artist on all parades except one, after she gave birth to her second child, and has been responsible for such stunning creations as the giant squid and Gilbert the turtle (who is probably Kerith's personal favourite).

Reflecting on those ten parades, Kerith says it's easy to see how the parade has grown and developed. "The way people have reacted to it has changed, in the way that it has completely embedded itself in the community as a thing that everybody does every year. Only in the last two or three years has it become a 'this is a thing we do' event. Until then it was a new thing."

Like other lead artists, she sees the same people return year after year and enjoys the buzz as parade day draws nearer. "I think people have got used to the chaos now. They know what to expect. They know the general materials and techniques we use. They've learnt to just let go and it doesn't matter actually what the finished product looks like. It doesn't matter that they may not be particularly good at art or they don't know how to use the tools. That's not a problem. What matters is people being here building things, being a part of it."

Kerith is keen to stress that she's there to help other people develop as makers. "My job is as a participatory artist. I'm here to let other people make things. We put in place stuff to help people come here and explore their own creativity, to make their own things and do their own work. My job isn't to make stuff for people.

"When I see my section ready to head off on parade day, that's my job done. Personally, I'm not a performer. The parade itself is kind of a by-product of what happens here, in this building, three or four weeks before a parade. The workshops are the parade to me. All the people in this building making things. That's where all the good stuff happens."

But she acknowledges that seeing people react to her big makes and hearing their comments is a wonderful thing on parade day. "You spend so much time and effort making something and you see what's gone wrong or what you haven't managed to finish. You see the bits where you've run out of time, money and brains. But people who see it for the first time don't see it like that. They just say, 'wow, that's amazing. Look at that squid.' Little kids' reactions are great because they don't know they're not real and that's lovely."

2015

Come Fly with Us!

Produced by Handmade Parade CIC

Director: Andrew Kim

Lead Artists: Kerith Ogden, Fran Sierevogel, Sue Walpole

Event Producer: Jude Wadley

The sky was the limit for the eighth annual parade. The first section, led by Kerith Ogden, featured bugs, dragonflies and butterflies. There was wind sock laundry on the line and a squad of stilt-walkers and drummers as the coming storm.

Aliens and astronauts featured in Fran Sierevogel's section. Fran made a rocket ship that 'launched' several times along the parade route. This year's donation collectors were fancy pigeons. In the final section of the parade, designed by Sue Walpole, there were aviators, airplanes, flying carpets, owls and fantastical birds. The parade ended with giant puppets by Thingumajig Theatre: three Sun Birds and a huge eagle with a six-metre wing span—at times a challenge on Hebden Bridge's narrow streets!

We had a great crew assisting us from Liverpool Institute for Performing Arts: Sophie Bursnoll, Heledd Rees and Jasmine Swan. Parade music was provided by Handmade Samba, Drum Machine, Skiband, Les Panards Dansants, Peace Artistes and Juba do Leão.

Reaching out to the whole community Sue Walpole

SUE'S FIRST INVOLVEMENT with the Handmade Parade came through the outreach programme that's such an important part of the parade. The aim has always been to get people involved with the parade – especially those who may otherwise not have taken part.

However, reaching those people and overcoming their initial reservations isn't always easy. Sue explained: "It can be really challenging for those people who are here as part of the outreach programme. It's not something that they've naturally come to of their own accord. But when they've been a part of the parade, they feel so proud of what they've achieved and learnt through that experience. Often it's something that they didn't think would be possible for them. They never thought they'd be able to create such amazing artwork.

"The parade brings people together and pushes people's creativity. People in outreach often say they can't do art and were told in school they were no good. It's about breaking down those barriers and creating amazing things."

Over the years, the parade has sent artists to schools and elderly people's centres and partnered with organisations such as Creative Minds, an NHS Foundation Trust that provides community, mental health and learning disability services. Sue has worked with a broad mix of people, including young carers, mental health service users and elderly people.

Seeing the positive benefits the parade has brought to a wide variety of people has been one of the many highlights for Sue. And having spent the last few years as a section leader for the parade, the sense of achievement on parade day is just as strong.

"When you turn around and see the parade coming towards you and you see all the small components come together to create the big picture, it's just really magical. And seeing how all your ideas have worked out larger than life and being together with all the people who have made that happen.

"My role in the workshops is to inspire people, letting them bring out their own ideas, maybe giving them a starter and going from there. I love seeing families coming together and making things and discovering new things in a new environment. This year, there was a brother and sister and an amazed parent absolutely goggle-eyed that they were working happily together. Those are the magic moments."

2016

Muck In!

Produced by Handmade Parade CIC

Director: Andrew Kim

Lead Artists: Kerith Ogden, Fran Sierevogel, Sue Walpole

Guest Artists: Tyran (Sergey Korsakov), Olesya Kandalintseva, Alena Gromova, Timofei Moskovkin, Plamen Radev Georgiev from Cardboardia (Russia and Bulgaria)

Event Producer: Jude Wadley

ALMOST EXACTLY SIX MONTHS to the day after the Boxing Day flood, the ninth annual parade took place with the theme Muck In!, a mythical retelling of the story of the floods and all those who mucked in to help the town emerge from the mess.

Our Spark Day was only a couple of months after the flood and, when we gathered our community, the flood and the enormous energy of the town coming together to clean up and rebuild seemed like the only theme possible for this year.

The parade started with a haunting flood siren followed by mud zombies, hippos and a dung beetle by Kerith Ogden. Thanks to a co-commission from the Yorkshire Festival, this was followed by a section by our guest company Cardboardia, whose members came from Russia, Bulgaria, Italy, Ireland and UK. This included a giant walking toilet machine and a tree that transformed waste to an alternative future.

Fran Sierevogel made a queen bee to lead her section of busy bees, worker ants and building beavers to help clean up the mess. Sue Walpole's giant sun and sun warriors led the final section in a celebration of a town that emerged from the floods, hand in hand, stronger and brighter than before.

A parade without borders
Spyros Andreopoulos

OVER THE PAST TEN PARADES, Hebden Bridge has played host to visiting artists from many countries including Russia, Bulgaria, Greece, Ireland, Italy, Spain, Denmark, Sweden, the Czech Republic, United States and Korea. They bring their skills, creativity and cultural influences to the parade and take home fresh ideas and skills they've picked up from the parade's own artists – along with many wonderful memories.

The guest artists have added an international flavour to the parade and helped to spread the message far and wide about what Hebden Bridge has created.

Spyros Andreopoulos, of Motus Terrae in Greece, is the latest guest artist to have brought his talents to the Handmade Parade.

He said: "We were honoured to be invited to this year's Handmade Parade to be in charge of creating some strange moments before the parade. We were working with a street theatre ensemble, creating a short performance to precede the parade and were also working on the stilt workshops, helping to introduce some new material.

"It's really an amazing place, not only Hebden Bridge but the working space for the Handmade Parade. It's a beautiful place to be and we see how the people are really part of it. It's not like they're guests. They know their way around, and feel really happy to create with the Handmade Parade team, and indeed us. Actually it felt like home for us from day one. People opened their arms and welcomed us."

Spyros believes art has a vital role to play in helping to build bridges between different people and countries at a time when division is rife. He explained: "I think bringing communities together is one of the most important things that art can do. At the moment we're going through some difficult times all over the world. Greece and the UK face different problems but there are a lot of similarities and personally, I think that art could be an answer to how to get people together and share and co-create.

"Eventually it will be one of the best ways to make people not afraid anymore, especially when you're working in public spaces and inviting people to see things from a different perspective. People can feel that this is their home and they have every right to ask questions about what's happening in their town and further afield. What Handmade Parade is doing in Hebden Bridge is exactly that. People are really connected with what is happening in the public spaces and the whole town is connected by what has been created.

"What we have in common is the need for sharing and getting together. That's the number one need for everyone, and we're using art as the medium to get together and to share. We're not only sharing ideas and inspiration, but also everyday life moments and getting to know each other, and that means that there are no boundaries. I was really glad to meet people from all over the world in Hebden Bridge. People from Syria, a colleague who is half-Greek half-Japanese, that's amazing. So, yeah, the Handmade Parade workshops are a place that people from everywhere can meet and co-create."

2017
Sea of Dreams

Produced by Handmade Parade CIC

Director: Andrew Kim

Lead Artists: Kerith Ogden, Fran Sierevogel, Sue Walpole

Guest Artists: Spyros Andreopoulos, Eduoard Georgiou from Motus Terrae (Greece)

Project Manager: Suzy Russell

Event Producer: Daisy Lee

WE VOYAGED on the Sea of Dreams for our tenth annual Hebden Bridge Handmade Parade. The parade pace was set by lifeguards. In the first section, Kerith Ogden's design took us to the seashore: fisher-folk fishing for dreams and wishes, hermit crabs lovingly carrying their homes on their backs and the Seagull, a rock pool band complete with drum kit, electric guitars and lots of air guitars.

In Sue Walpole's second section, we went deep into the sea to find dead sea kelp, sleepwalkers with their dreams stuck in the tentacles of jellyfish and a giant octopus and skeleton fish with trawler nets.

In the last section, led by Fran Sierevogel, we woke from this nightmare to find each other and set sail towards our dreams: ships decorated with family portraits (all drawn by workshop participants) and the important objects we take with us on our journeys, families of seahorses, dolphin companions and Arctic terns with suitcases.

We hosted two artists from Greece's Motus Terrae, who taught stilt-walking and organised a street theatre ensemble that created encounters and games as the audience waited for the parade.

This year, we had a fantastic set of interns who have worked with us most of the year: Govi Asano, Sandra McCracken, Rose Revitt and Rowan Taylor.

Valley of Lights and Lamplighter Festival

IN 2012, following the flooding in our valley, we decided to do something that would help boost local businesses and demonstrate the renewed vibrancy of our communities. We partnered with Totally Locally, a social enterprise and shop local movement, to create a series of evening events in three of our towns, Todmorden, Hebden Bridge and Mytholmroyd.

Each town had a series of lantern-making workshops and each town had a festival night with a lantern parade, a fire pageant, illuminated street acts, lots of street bands and a night market. It was the first time our company had produced a night time event and it felt right. The response was tremendous and we enjoyed the creative challenge of making events with the night as our backdrop. It immediately felt like a good balance for us to have another local event on the opposite side of the year from the Hebden Bridge Handmade Parade.

Based on the success of Valley of Light, the following year, we decided to create a new event based in Todmorden, just five miles up the valley from Hebden Bridge, called the Lamplighter Festival. Now in its fifth year, the festival is focused on the Lamplighter, an

exquisite lantern puppet by Kerith Ogden, who returns once a year to walk the streets of Todmorden to share her light with us as we head into the darkest time of the year.

We hold two weeks of free lantern-making workshops (donations welcome) in Todmorden and offer fire spinning workshops and outreach workshops where artists work with groups to create illuminated installations. The festival includes a lantern parade, fire and illuminated installations, street bands, street theatre and street food. From the beginning, we've shaped this festival as a showcase for local outdoor arts, with virtually all of those involved based in the upper Calder Valley.

Before we started producing winter events, most of the team only came together for a couple of months a year. With our lantern events, our parade art and workshops became more in demand throughout the year. In the last few years, we've grown to have a year-round team producing our signature events and also creating Handmade Parade events throughout the UK and beyond.

Parading the North

HANDMADE PARADE was originally the name of Hebden Bridge's midsummer parade, produced by HEADS and Thingumajig Theatre. In 2009, when HEADS, a participatory arts organisation, decided to close its doors, we decided to form a new company to make sure our parade could continue. This was called Handmade Parade CIC (Community Interest Company).

As the photos, videos and word of mouth about the style and quality of participation in our parades started to spread, other events began to approach us about bringing our parade art to their community.

In 2015, with support from Arts Council England, we turned our attention to the infrastructure of our company and made the investment in growing the company to support year-round delivery that would allow us to better support our artists and our artistic developments.

We enlisted an Executive Director, Kathleen McGrath, and a Development Manager, Kay King.

With this backbone of administrative and developmental support, and with the tireless efforts of our committed board of directors, we have been able to sustainably grow our work. Handmade Parade has become something of a 'lab for learning' for other community groups and leaders as well as for arts organisations across the globe. In 2017, we delivered a year-long programme called 'Parading the North'.

Parading the North has seen the company solidify, consolidate, and further share our approach. It has allowed us to focus on three strategic areas – parade events, training and development and social impact. We are looking carefully at the need and methods for audience development and evaluation within parading events and recognise our responsibility to a national parade art agenda that complements our local community.

We have developed and delivered our first year of our parade artists' training programme and now offer an annual opportunity for eight emerging parade artists to undertake extensive, bespoke training within the company which contributes to job creation in the sector.

We have become leaders in sharing our work, delivering events that bring together cohorts of parade art companies to co-deliver and present work for new audiences and to strengthen the image and collective energy of parade efforts in the North of England.

We have worked with communities across the UK and beyond to deliver parades for Yorkshire Festival, Skipton Puppet Festival, Hepworth Wakefield Gallery, Fleetwood Festival of Transport, Manchester Day Parade, Just So Festival, Kendal Calling, Bluedot Festival, Ramsgate Festival, Holmfirth Arts Festival and lantern parades in Knutsford, Otley, Tameside, Elland and Light Night Leeds. We created parades for Hull City of Culture and Lancashire Encounters' Brief Encounters in Preston, both of which involved costume-making, bespoke giant puppets and teaching and creating a new stilt ensemble with local youths. We've created a 5.5 metre lantern giant to help reopen Oldham Old Town Hall and a giant David Hockney puppet, leading a sausage

dog parade, to mark his 80th birthday.

In 2016, we created our first overseas event: a lantern parade in Pangyo, South Korea. In 2017, our 10th year, we taught masterclasses in Svendborg (Denmark) and Derry (Northern Ireland) and collaborated with Namoodak Movement Lab near Cheongsong, South Korea to create a series of eight village lantern parades welcoming the arrival of the Apple Goddess. Coming up, we will be helping to create a Handmade Parade style parade in Bulgaria as part of Plovdiv 2019 European Capital of Culture.

Although we are still very much rooted in creating the space to deepen the creativity in our local and regional communities, we are enjoying the journey of spiraling outwards and taking the hands of partners who create the space in their own communities for this joyful dance.

Photo credits

Page 3: Design and Green Man by Fran Sierevogel; photo by Ian Hodgson

Page 4: Design by Kerith Odgen; photo by Graham Wynne

Page 7: Andrew Kim with his musk ox; photo by Ian Hodgson

Page 8: Ruth Richardson and her net of dreams and memories; photo by Darren Fleming

Page 11: Alison Duddle's Water Bearers; photo by Ian Hodgson

Page 12: Ships by Jonny Quick; photo by Nigel Hillier. Umbrella section by Andrew Kim; photo by Ian Hodgson. Rain Queen by Andrew Kim; photo by Nigel Hillier. Geese pace makers Kathy and Michelle; photo by Nigel Hillier.

Page 13: Heron by Kerith Ogden; photo by Ian Hodgson

Page 14: Swimmer by Andrew Kim; photo by Nigel Hillier

Page 15: Jonny Quick as head pirate; photo by Nigel Hillier. Ships photo by Chris Ratcliffe. Water Bearers by Alison Duddle; photo by Nigel Hillier. Water birds design by Kerith Ogden; photo by Chris Ratcliffe.

Page 16: Photo by Nigel Hillier

Page 17: Jude Wadley photo by Ian Hodgson

Page 19: Alison Duddle's Queen Bee; photo by Ian Hodgson

Page 20: Photos by Nigel Hillier

Page 21: Carnival Crew Tees Valley; photo by Nigel Hillier

Page 22: Photos by Nigel Hillier and Ian Hodgson

Page 23: Photos by Nigel Hillier (left) and Ian Hodgson (2 on right)

Page 24: Photo by Ian Hodgson

Page 25: Photo of Mitch Oldham by Craig Shaw

Page 27: Photo by Craig Shaw

Page 28: Car, feet by Theo Wickenden; photo by Ian Hodgson. Lower left photo by Craig Shaw. Stilt geese by Alison Duddle, masked character by Soozin Hirschmugl; photo by Ian Hodgson. Squid by Kerith Ogden; photo by Ian Hodgson.

Page 29: Sun Birds by Thingumajig Theatre; photo by Ian Hodgson

Pages 30 and **31**: Photos by Ian Hodgson

Page 33: Big mouth by Jonny Quick; photo by Ian Hodgson

Page 34: Skiband photo by Craig Shaw. Top right and bottom row photos by Ian Hodgson; Plucky the giant chicken by Thingumajig Theatre

Page 35: Fishmonger by Andrew Kim; photo by Craig Shaw

Page 36: Left and top right photos by Ian Hodgson; lower right photo by Darren Fleming

Page 37: Louise Heppleston's photo by Ian Hodgson

Page 39: Autumn leaf dragon by Andrew and Kathy Kim; photo by Darren Fleming

Page 40: Prince Charles greets director Andrew Kim; photo by Nigel Hillier. Lower left and right photos by Craig Shaw.

Page 41: Upper left by Ian Hodgson; lower right by Darren Flemming; all others by Craig Shaw

Page 42: Photo by Darren Fleming

Page 43: Left photos by Ian Hodgson: Kerith Ogden's stag photo by Craig Shaw

Page 44: Lisa Gort's hedgehog lends flooded shop owners a little support; photo by Ian Hodgson

Page 45: Linda Green photo by Ian Hodgson

Page 47: Photo by Ian Hodgson

Page 48: Photo by Ian Hodgson

Page 49: Left two photos by Ian Hodgson; upper right photo by Darren Fleming; lower right photo by Craig Shaw

Page 50: Section design by Lisa Gort; photo by Ian Hodgson

Page 51: Left: Brigid by Kerith Ogden; photo by Darren Fleming. Top right trolls by Duane Tougas; photo by Darren Fleming.

Pages 52 and 53: Photos of Ruth Richardson by Ian Hodgson

Pages 54 and 55: 2013 parade portraits by Steve Morgan

Page 57: Camel by Lisa Gort; photo by Darren Fleming

Page 58: Photo by Ian Hodgson

Page 59: Top left design by Fran Sierevogel; photo by Craig Shaw. Bottom left design by Andrew Kim; photo by Craig Shaw Right: Blue

Peter presenter Barney Harwood in front of Andrew Kim's musk ox; photo by Ian Hodgson.

Page 60: Section by Fran Sierevogel; photo by Craig Shaw

Page 61: Dodo by Thingumajig Theatre; photo by Graham Wynne. Elephant by Fran Sierevogel; photo by Darren Fleming. Bottom photos by Darren Fleming.

Page 62: Turtle by Kerith Ogden, structure by Ian Broscomb; photo by Craig Shaw.

Page 63: Kerith Ogden photo by Ian Hodgson

Page 65: Photo by Ian Hodgson

Page 66: Alien section by Fran Sierevogel; Eagle by Andrew Kim; Butterfly wings by Cabasa Carnival Arts; aeroplane section by Sue Walpole. Photos by Ian Hodgson.

Page 67: Dragonfly by Kerith Ogden; photo by Ian Hodgson; other photos by Craig Shaw

Page 68: Design by Sue Walpole; photo by Ian Hodgson

Page 69: Top left: design by Kerith Ogden; photo by Ian Hodgson. Bottom left and right photos by Craig Shaw.

Page 70: Creative Minds project photo by Jude Wadley

Page 71: Sue Walpole photo by Craig Shaw

Page 73: Section design by Sue Walpole; photo by Graham Wynne

Page 74: Section by Kerith Ogden; photo by Graham Wynne

Page 75: (left) Queen Bee and design by Fran Sierevogel; photo by Graham Wynne. Photos on right by Ian Hodgson; Earth Spirit by Thingumajig Theatre.

Page 76: Dung beetle by Kerith Ogden; top right: Cardboardia. All photos by Ian Hodgson.

Page 77: Mud bath by Kerith Odgen; photo by Ian Hodgson. Sun by Sue Walpole; photo by Graham Wynne. Queen Bee by Fran Sierevogel; photo by Ian Hodgson. Washing machine puppets by Charlie Smith; photo by Ian Hodgson.

Page 78: Cardboardia photo by Ian Hodgson

Page 79: Spyros Andreopolos photo by Darren Fleming

Page 81: Gil Burn's dance ensemble design by Kerith Ogden; photo by Craig Shaw.

Page 82: Sirens photo and Kerith Ogden's hermit crab photos by Darren Fleming. Fran Sierevogel's ship photo by Graham Wynne. Motus Terrae's sleepwalkers photo by Darren Fleming.

Page 83: Lifeguards photo by Craig Shaw. Ship section design by Fran Sierevogel, Shark by Rag and Bone; photo by Darren Fleming. Andrew Kim giant puppet workshop horses photo and Sue Walpole's octopus photos by Darren Fleming.

Page 84: Lamplighter by Kerith Ogden, orbs by Fran Sierevogel; photo by Craig Shaw

Page 86: FlameOz photo by Craig Shaw

Page 87: Jellyfish by Thingumajig Theatre; photo by Ian Hodgson

Page 88: Robot by Andrew Kim; photo by Ian Hodgson. Swan by Kerith Ogden; photo by Craig Shaw. Owl and Lamplighter by Kerith Ogden; photo by Ian Hodgson.

Page 89: Dragon by Leeway; photo by Ian Hodgson. Moon by Andrew Kim, Stars by Alison Duddle; photo by Craig Shaw. Bear by Adam Krátký and Dora Kratka; photo by Ian Hodgson. Floating flowers by Spacecadets; photo by Craig Shaw

Page 91: Rossington miners; photo by Craig Shaw. Robot by Andrew Kim; photo by Craig Shaw. David Hockney by Andrew Kim and Shipley Embroiderers' Guild; photo by Ian Hodgson. Oldham giant by Kerith Ogden and Ian Broscomb; photo by Ian Hodgson.

Page 92: Rossington Parade; photo by Craig Shaw. Fleetwood Festival of Transport float by Noah Rose and Sue Walpole; photo by Craig Shaw. Fantastical Cycle Parade wheelchairs led by Jude Wadley; photo by Ian Hodgson. Dragon for Pangyo Festival, Korea by Andrew Kim; photo by Dong-Heon Kang.

Page 93: David Hockney sausage dogs designed by Morwenna Catt; photo by Ian Hodgson. Dragonflies by Kerith Ogden for Skipton Puppet Festival; photo by Craig Shaw. Snail bikes by Andrew Kim for Fantastical Cycle Parade; photo by Ian Hodgson. Fish by Fran Sierevogel and Hermit crabs by Sue Walpole; photo by Romain Reglade.

Acknowlegements

Links

Handmade Parade:
handmadeparade.co.uk

Frogsdesign:
www.frogsdesign.co.uk

John Fox:
www.welfare-state.org
www.deadgoodguides.com

Photographers

Darren Fleming:
darrenflemingphotography.co.uk

Ian Hodgson:
www.ianhodgson.co.uk

Craig Shaw:
www.bluplanetphoto.co.uk

Graham Wynne:
www.grahamwynnephoto.com

Nigel Hillier:
archive.nigelhillier.com/index

Steve Morgan:
www.stevemorganphoto.co.uk

Chris Ratcliffe
www.hebdenbridge.co.uk

Handmade Parade CIC 2017 Team

Executive Director:
Kathleen McGrath

Artistic Director:
Andrew Kim

Project Managers/Lead Artists:
Kerith Ogden, Fran Sierevogel,
Sue Walpole

Development Manager:
Kay King

Community Engagement Manager:
Jude Wadley

**Hebden Parade/Lamplighter
Project Manager:**
Suzy Russell

**Hebden Parade/Lamplighter Event
Manager:**
Daisy Lee

Volunteer Coordinators:
Kate Rogers, Thea Soltau

Intern Coordinator:
Alison Duddle

Interns:
Govi Asano, Rose Revitt, Sandra
McCracken, Rowan Taylor

Thanks

We would like to thank the many artists, administrators and board of directors who have helped shape, sustain and grow our company especially Jude Wadley and Mel Rix, Rebecca Dearden, Hannah Merriman, Leisa Gray and Kathleen McGrath and past and present board of directors, especially our past chairs Linda Green, Liz Anstee and Pam Warhurst and our current board of directors: Alex Baldacci, Lynnette Crossley, Pete Gascoigne, Andrew Kim, Kathleen McGrath, Kerith Ogden, Dan Powers, Carol Stow and Pam Warhurst.

Huge hugs and thanks to the hundreds of volunteers who have made every one of our events possible.

Andrew would like to thank Kathy Kim for 10 years of steady behind-the-scenes never-would-have-happened-without-her support. He moved to England for love, only later to realise that if you hold love in the centre, everything is better and possible.

Funders

Our tenth year, including our 10th Hebden Bridge Handmade Parade, our 5th Lamplighter Festival, a year-round training programme and this publication, was made possible with the support of:

Arts Council England

Calderdale Council

Todmorden Town Council

Hebden Royd Town Council

Big Lottery Fund

Community Foundation for Calderdale

Creative Minds